Fort Lonesome

———

Timothy Krcmarik

FUTURECYCLE PRESS
www.futurecycle.org

Cover artwork, unattributed abstract painting from the public domain; author photo by Olive Gentry Metcalf; cover and interior book design by Diane Kistner; Caecilia text and titling

Library of Congress Control Number: 2019957902

Published by FutureCycle Press
Athens, Georgia, USA

ISBN 978-1-942371-95-3

for Jody and Wyatt

Contents

"The rabbits think I'm their god. Peaceful and loving," I said.
"Without rabbit stew you are nothing," she said.

—James Tate

Dunkleosteus

Consider yourself counted,
sister bluebird, chirping for crumbs
on the street of white marble

between my coffee and cigarettes,
little lost Gretel
singing for your supper

while Hansel hides above us
holding his stomach
in the canopy's deep dark green.

Though what do I know?
I don't speak bluebird.
You might just as well be your species'

Amazon Queen
throwing down a tiny silver gauntlet,
prophesying the day your kind

will force us back under the rock
from whence we came,
or Joan of Arc

ordering your legions forward
while I sit here
stirring sugar absently

into a double espresso,
trying to remember
what I was just thinking about and why.

Wrist

This morning has opened
with such technical precision,
moon gathering its star charts and astrolabe,

sun tapping the horizon
with its scarlet baton
as though it spent all night

on the other side of the world
fussing over the symphony
of silent winter brilliance,

which I am attending alone
in a rumpled sweatshirt
and white cotton Fruit of the Looms.

And aside from the leaded windows
honeycombed with frost, the cardinal
shivering like a match strike in the snow-crowned oak,

there is nothing else to add
about the morning
or about my sweatshirt for that matter

with its frayed collar and bone-shaped hole
near the wrist, except
that it has a large bird of prey on the front

wearing a letterman's sweater,
curling its flight feathers into fists,
and looking very much like something

in the Natural History Museum
who
for the soft miracles of heart and mind

once hunted our ancestors
to near extinction
many thousands of miles to the East.

Futon

This town is famous for its old courthouse,
a Greek Revival affair
of brick and granite with tall white pillars

and a ghost pacing the clock tower
to remind everybody
just how slowly the wheels of Justice turn.

And there are many truths to be discovered
by sitting quietly in its shadow
as dusk settles on the statue of Progress,

the copper-colored trees,
meditating on its stately face
as though it held any power at all

compared to the bachelorette party
revving its engines in the nearby tavern
with straight whiskey and a colorful toast

for technological supremacy
to the chrome and silicone penises
waiting faithfully

in their purses and bedside drawers,
the impeccable understudies
ready to pinch hit for their unzenithed lovers

represented here, collectively, by a shapeless futon
eating taco crumbs
from its own hairy navel,

a futon flightless enough to make Creation,
already much harangued
by another long day at the forge,

light the lamp at Her heavy drafting table
and sigh like an anvil to unfurl
the scroll of our universe once again

as She draws a pencil,
one of the really sharp ones,
from their star-blackened cup.

Moon

To the man strolling down a quiet street
watching it rise slowly
through pipe smoke and icy branches

it may be the candle of higher thought
or a lover's flaxen hair.
The cop padding along her beat

on broken arches
might feel its cratered mug
is the walleyed gaze of the security state

while the priest crumbled by his confessional
can see only a dumpster fire
scattering the roaches of human error.

You may already know the moon
is sugar to the sweet tooth,
the heart of the melting snowman,

and the escaped convict's midnight train,
but are you aware it is the fern-kissed pool
of the narcissist, the astrologer's cataract,

the cherry of a post-coital cigarette?
Are you aware it is the werewolf's chalice,
the beggar's golden ticket,

and the hard nipple's dollop of wild honey?
I could go on until sunrise
reminding you the moon

is a ten-pound pearl to the jeweler,
a pillow to the insomniac,
the prankster's fanny

waving from the window of a passing car,
but we'd only end up arguing
whether or not it is cream in the cat's bowl,

the orphan's mother, or a deathbed pendulum.
Just know that for me and everyone else
riding a hot city bus early one night in June

the moon is the Mayor's beacon,
thousands of lumens per square foot
summoning a large animate pie

to march down the aisle
and sock two mouthy gun nuts
right in their twisted kissers

with its great big whipped cream fist,
cleansing them of bitterness,
flinging open the shutters of their hearts,

and later,
after a journey of unexpected romance and pursuit,
officiating their wedding

at the small organic vineyard
they've established in Sonoma,
fire in the hearthstone, babies on the way.

Wanderer

We were sharing a bottle of wine after dinner,
napkins crumpled on the tablecloth,
the shin bone of a lamb

floating in a pool of butter on each plate,
when I joked,
and I *was* joking,

that your reasonable views
on the patriarchy
were classic symptoms of wandering womb.

Your womb, I laughed, never being one
to dig myself out of a hole,
wandering like a hobo,

riding the rails with a whistle on her lips
and a tin of beans in her bindle,
pink face flush with sunlight,

fallopian tubes
waving like pigtails in the breeze,
all of which you rebuffed with frankness

like a bullet
zipping through a book of love poems,
shattering a vase of roses,

winging poor Cupid like a migratory loon.
And every woman
locked between those leather covers

descending an ivy-covered tower
to gather at an old pond
in the snowy wilds of the margins

where a frog native to those clear black waters,
a rare species of male,
wanders the icy depths,

mouth filled with the eggs of his lover
that he will carry in hunger
until the children are born.

Physical

In a volley of baseball scores
and sideways rain,
word comes trembling through the pines,

crackling down the wire,
that astronomers have unearthed
the lowest note in the universe,

a B-flat 57 octaves below
the piano's middle C.
Older than sunlight, they say,

and droning bluely from a black hole
at the heart of the Perseus Cluster,
which, I tell my harmonica,

fitting her familiar lips to mine,
can only mean
that across this inconstant blossom

of stellar nurseries,
hidden in the grand dark garden
of physical mystery, that black hole's

lover
is lying in some other black hole's arms,
their cigarette catching the sheets on fire,

the lacework drapes,
and before you know it,
because such is the nature of fire,

the Dipper in its starry cauldron,
the Archer at his war dance,
the Great Bear rising from a winter's sleep.

Europa

As you tiptoe like a Buddha
over the crooked footpath of my vertebrae,
sipping your coffee and setting

my serpentine back to rights,
I am sprawled out like Prometheus
on the piney floorboards,

groveling with mammalian relief
as though Hercules just
broke my chains on Mount Caucasus

and tore both wings from the eagle
come to gorge on my liver.
So you would hardly guess

I'm doing my best Orpheus,
praising all you will do today to keep
a steady trickle of children

from disappearing down the free world's
victim-to-prisoner pipeline.
But if you can somehow manage

to tune out the makeshift reconstruction
of my neural highway
and fix your ears to sparrows crooning

or the soughing hackberry trees,
then you will hear the pillars of heaven
crack with yearning

as I sing this song of social workers.
You will hear the wet cliffs
and every salt-scrubbed dune

gasp in windblown astonishment
as the god of gods himself,
having assumed the guise of a white bull

and kidnapped a young beauty,
meaning to rape her repeatedly on Crete,
looks back over his shoulder

through the sea foam and curling waves
to where you are stepping from the beach
in hawkeyed pursuit,

making him snort in horror
at the increasing possibility
that he's no kind of god at all.

Des Plaines

Okay, so it's hardly the Thames
on whose outer banks Shakespeare
thumbed his nose at Puritans and plague,

nor is it the Danube immortalized by Strauss
as both beautiful *and* blue.
No foundling will suckle its muddy dugs

as Romulus nursed the Tiber
before knifing his brother and inventing Rome,
and let's not bet the farm

it will host any sort of history,
Washington crossing the Delaware,
Grant wresting the Mississippi from Lee.

It is possible lovers lie in the shade
of its many sycamore trees
as Parisians laze by the Seine

sighing at the currents of time
or the heart's taste for blood,
but one is likely a prostitute,

their love a routine transaction,
and both have an eye out for the fuzz.
Honestly, if it's the cradle of civilization you're after,

head for the Tigris and Euphrates,
or the Amazon if pink dolphins and the green
lungs of the world are more your speed.

The Snake if you feel like dying.
The Nile if you've got a good one for the Sphinx.
Because here is only the dark ribbon of my youth,

a small tributary winding into the wilder
rivers of Thought and Memory,
though not without swelling every spring

to fill the basement with fertile,
radioactive slime. Mother drinking whiskey.
Father ripping out his hair. And, hey, there's me

grunting up the rickety staircase
with an old plaid sofa on my shoulders
then racing back down to save

the beanbag chairs and lava lamps,
the Nintendo and color TV,
all the sacred totems of Make-out City.

Americano

What is there to do when you hear
the Immortals turn slowly
in their marble beds below the *Colle Palatino*

to watch a portly tourist family
puff heavenward
in identical silk Hawaiian shirts

and tallyho one another
in the sturdy, snowplow dialect
of central Minnesota

but take another sip
from your little espresso cup
and savor the unlikely marriage

of earth and sugar therein? What
but to lean back in one of the spindly
iron chairs under the café's awning,

letting the sun light your cranium
and Rome go on
insisting it is the Eternal City—

a conjecture so outlandish,
what is there to do
atop these seven hills of Aeneas

but order an Americano
and massage your pregnant wife's sore feet
after marching her

from the dust of one civilization
towards the ashes of the next,
letting her pleasure dignify this mutable life

of good acts and pointless virtue
you two crazy kids
are so intent on building together.

Struggle

Sunflowers crowd the long
strip of light
between the tree line and the house.

They are so tall in June
it will take two of me,
one standing on the other's shoulders,

to study their dark faces,
one me wallowing like a honeybee,
the other me crumbling under the weight.

Themes

They are everywhere all at once
and all the time,
the seasons whirling mosslessly along,

the darkness doing its dust-devil tango
with the light.
And I, of sound bookwormfulness,

can't kick a pebble without pelting one,
Innocence playing speed chess with Experience,
True Love rowing Bitter Regret

in a swan-shaped boat,
as though the world was a shadow-lantern
turned inside out

and I was standing perfectly still,
blank as a canvas
at its beating black center,

letting the spectrum of human desires
glide through me
like sunbeams slowed imperceptibly

on their single-minded commute
across the Universe,
the Rise to Power alley-oop dunking,

the Fall of Empires whiffing at the plate,
or the theme of this poem,
which has slipped these fingers

and finned madly upstream
to spawn with other themes in the waters of their birth
before I can fry it up in a five-paragraph essay

with topic sentences, supporting evidence,
and a smooth transition
into whatever comes next.

Icon

In the fifteen-second span it took
to stretch two hundred feet of hose
down the berth of a burning bungalow,

accompanied the livelong way
by a small boy skipping with his mutt
and cheerfully ignoring

my profanity-laced imploring
to go play somewhere faraway
like an active volcano or the ocean floor,

I might just as well have stood there
sermonizing on the supple grace
of origami swans

for what little good my words did
to sway that kid and his ragamuffin pal
from the closest they'd yet come

to the miraculous and terrible.
They were wholly satisfied to stand
not six feet back in mortal danger

and watch me kick the back door open,
tongues of fire roiling
off the windows and the eaves.

And had you met their eyes just then,
you would have seen them brimming
with the iconic stuff

of epic poems and comic books,
nothing like the cruel, misshapen thing
they loathed forevermore

when I grabbed them by the scruffs
and flung them over a fence
with a gruff, Get lost!

some bridge troll sent to wreck the lives
of dogs and children, some ogre
best imprisoned at the center of the earth.

Tsunami

I am not to be counted today
among the lovers
of sunny Latin maxims,

that carefree lot nibbling each other
in broom closets and backrooms
the world over

or clop-clopping down their secret beaches
on prissy alabaster stallions.
No climber of frozen waterfalls

squinting through the blizzard
of her own frozen tears
will think of me

kneeling here on all fours in the kitchen,
fishing around a rusty green toolbox
for a monkey wrench,

and muster such grit to conquer the face
of Old Man Winter.
Poets will not sing of the way

I dislocate a pinkie,
nor painters capture the tsunami
rushing from my tear ducts

as whirlwinds of vulgarity
twist my lips in a knot
and gobble everything in their path,

because this is the other kind of day
(when rain won't glaze the red wheelbarrow
nor the white chickens stand beside it just so),

the kind that will simply have
to seize itself
no matter what Horace will think

should he appear suddenly out of thin air,
flabbergasted by the wonders
of modern refrigeration

if less so by the pale plumber's crack
peeking over the dark blue horizon
of my jeans.

Nothing

said I had passed on my genes
and was now quite worthless to the tribe
like stepping into the ditch

beside a lonesome highway
and sinking to my balls
in cold wet mud,

tire iron swallowed by cattails,
donut floating merrily towards the sea,
and life hanging on the hope

some helpful soul would pass by
before wolves arrived
or dehydration planted me

face first into the song
of a thousand horny toads,
there to become one of those bog people

peat farmers dig up,
tanned as shoe leather,
boneless as a balloon.

And it turned out Hope
was an exuberantly foul-mouthed trucker
with ten kids and cirrhosis,

a trove of dirty jokes and weeks to live.
His name was Chuy
and by now he is stardust or worm food,

but if it were up to me,
he'd be the broke-beak grackle
terrorizing the shellac-haired youth

of this crowded bistro
with her gutful of poetry
while the kids languish

to immortalize their brunch
as though the world turns
on pictures

of house-cured pastrami omelets
and organic whiskey cocktails,
local chicharrones and cornichons.

Modern

Usually, the Tyrannosaurus Rex
on my son's thin pajama shirt
is laudably chipper for six a.m.,

surfing down a rainbow
before the rest of us have had a chance
to scratch our fannies or rub the sleep

from our bloodshot eyes, but this morning
something was eerily different
in the way he gazed out

across the rim of his dark aviators,
something hair-raisingly askew,
as I drew the shirt over Wyatt's head,

that made it seem the Ghost of Cretaceous-
Paleogene Past had come to rattle
heavy chains of warning,

albeit with a pair of tiny green arms.
Or the Ghost of Anthropocene Future,
I thought later this gusty April day

as letters dropped through the mail slot
and I poured myself another cup
of coal-black giddyup, setting aside

the sonnet I've been lately mulling
about two lovers slipping on the same
banana peel, to consider Homo sapiens

pried from the fossil record ages hence
and silkscreened on cotton jammies
that some exotic life-form will slide off

the many wriggling appendages
of its bioluminescent pride-and-joy,
wondering if there is milk in the fridge,

bread in the pantry or butter,
not thinking at all about the hamper
or the modern hominid inside

walking naked across a desert plain,
glancing back at footprints he is leaving
in the softly snowing volcanic ash.

Brueghel

I beg your pardon, abs,
for the bustling coral reef
I paid some unsung Brueghel

to paint there until the day my body
should recommence with earth,
and excuse me, chest,

for the mermaids
bathing coyly
under the sun and moon

on either shoulder.
Arms, mea culpa for the grocery list
of symbols usurped

from the world's First Peoples,
and, neck, have mercy
for the name-glutted heart

where each bitter mistress
is stricken
by a thin black adder.

Because, honestly, what is that
compared to the wolf-riddled darkness
howling down my back

like a river of distilled terror
or the rainforest
stretching belly button to big toe

and crowned by a toucan
saluting all of Creation with his beak?
Face, old pal,

you've never been much to look at,
but as I sit on this park bench
watching a row of fuzzy ducklings

waddle smartly after their mother
onto the polished lens of the pond,
I hardly think that justifies

having stamped a clown's wide grimace
on what was
and what may yet be pristine wilderness.

Paperboy

The crick in my limbs and lower back
after a full day planting petunias
has gone from world-weary baritone

to soprano unhinged,
so that, at day's end, kneeling upright
from the gardener's mendicant stoop

takes a great deal of time and groaning,
though not so much time nor,
probably, groaning,

as the light of that first star took
to reach the earth and burn through
the hubris of our sleepless city

like a paperboy having loaded his satchel
early one morning thirty-three million
years ago,

downing a slice of burnt bacon,
a mug of tea with plenty of milk and sugar,
and his mother waving from the porch

as he raced off
down a Main Street of endless night
lest he should be late delivering

to a man in a flowerbed
grinning at an alien sky
the bright evening news of himself.

Otitis Media

A germ has bedded flocks in his middle ear
like inhospitable Polyphemus.
Go now, Amoxicillin, with wine and spear
under the banners of Odysseus.

Or take Hermes' stone and blather should these
prove best to shut the cretin's Argus eyes
and scatterbrain our baby's nemesis
with that hard dose of crafty lullabies.

Schnoz

You've probably never heard of John Donne,
mosquito biting my forehead
on this bright and balmy day in late October,

because your kind doesn't much go in for books,
let alone poetry,
let alone metaphysical love poetry

of early seventeenth-century Britain,
but he wrote a very famous poem
where this guy is trying to sleep with this girl,

and they're both crawling with fleas,
so he points to one and essentially says,
"Look, if that flea bites us

and our blood mingles in its belly,
that's not Sin,
that's Nature,

and since the flea
is like our love, it's only natural
we should bite one another

until we're mostly dead of pleasure."
And that's how poets got laid in the olden days
and how fleas

sort of ran things from the shadows.
But whereas we moderns wash our linens
and strive

to keep our bits and pieces parasite free,
you are worthless as a device
for sexual overture.

So, enjoy whatever magic
you've witched
from my consciousness,

wildcatting around my frontal lobe
with that promiscuous hypodermic
you call a schnoz,

because I'm about to mash you back
to basic elements
and your girlfriend

competing for the breasts
my wife has dipped so generously
to my open mouth

in a poem
3 billion years old
and still able to entertain us.

Monk

Standing on the mailbox,
face to the lashing rains of late October,
is a green fellow with a white breast,

a monk parakeet, I discover,
thumbing through a guide of North American birds,
famous with city dwellers

for its power to salve loneliness with song and wit
though defectors such as this
have returned to life beyond the gilded cage

with its water bowl and seed dish,
its shredded obituaries spread across the floor.
And beyond that, the book-lined study

with its leaded windows and marble mantle,
its ashtray on a brass side table
next to a gooseneck lamp and deep leather chair.

You can keep your pheasant roasting in the oven,
he seems to say, turning his back to me
as a hard sleet begins,

your candles flickering at the long wooden table,
your glass full of earthy red wine.
To say nothing of white tulips in a glass vase

or the zinc sideboard where a loaf of bread
is lying next to a wedge of cheese, a bunch of grapes, and a knife.
The violin lying on the sofa.

The sheaf of papers and pen.
All of it,
his utter indifference to the elements proclaims,

just one more iron link
in a life chained to fleeting desires
right down

to the fragrant chunk of pine
I toss onto the fire
my wife and I will lie in front of tonight.

And what will he think then? I ask the raven
sitting on my shoulder,
though I already know what that one's going to say.

Spandex

To the slow parade of strollers
passing by Engine 16 this drizzly afternoon
I must look like a braying jackass,

flipping this giant tractor tire
up and down the street
like it's a chocolate donut for Cronus

or King Kong's lost pinky ring;
and if not a braying jackass,
then like some doughy Hercules

grappling his life away in lesser combat
with stubborn love handles
and a paunch rising like the summer moon;

and if not some doughy Hercules,
then perhaps like nothing more
than an aging civil servant

taking in the tea-weak sunshine
and propping himself up
against his own natural decline

unless you're the curvaceous
creampuff
who just jogged up Cullen Avenue

in black spandex and hot pink sweat bands,
grinned with pure sex
and catcalled, "Lookin' good, Fireman!"

In which case, thank you
for invigorating the Beautiful Ideal forever
and spurring the scar tissue

in the temples of my weathered injuries
to grab hold of little Olympic bars
and begin deadlifting, an act

that has nothing to do with the dead
nor disturbing their slumber
on the grassy commons of eternity.

Late One Night in Verona

The osteria we *just had to try*
was stuffed with ribald Tybalts wall to wall
and one unwelcome Mercutio hawking

painted roses at two measly euros
a pop. The blotto crowd jeered him with a squall
of florid arias, their squalid squawking

swelling in spite until the harried owner
expelled him to the night's expunging tide
of anonymous violence and murder.

Or not so anonymous, Love conjectured,
her amore set thoughtfully aside
that we should explore trafficked foreigners

indentured to mafia-backed debt
and dumped sometimes at the house of Capulet.

La Jolla

If I find myself choking on rage
as a bronzed beach harpy sideswipes me
doing eighty through the crosswalk

and floors it for La Jolla
in her half-million-dollar streak
of lightning and sperm,

it is because up in my brain's
Bureau of Comebacks and Retorts—
behind a door with a paper sign

that reads, *Geniuses at work!*—
a bunch of unpaid interns
are ignoring the red alert

from my mouth for an insult
capable of melting the human ego,
flicking paper footballs instead

or doodling some sort of flimsy
intraoffice Kama Sutra,
because they've read the company handbook,

which clearly states that although Management
understands timing is everything,
"employees shall not rush perfection

in all matters of poetry
but practice mastering silence
until said poetry is potent enough

to make a lover
tear the pants from one's body
in a fit of wine and candlelight

as lily wounds of night
lap at the western sky's thin tongues
of fiery dominion."

Oh

She must have seen the storm clouds
swirling around my head,
the orthopedist wrapping my wrist

in layers of wet fiberglass,
when she rolled her eyes like a teenager
asked to have opinions

about iambic pentameter or democracy
and said, "Oh, it's not the end of the world."
Not *Oh* the way a poet would say it

at the sight of a naked lover or passing hearse,
but *Oh* the way your meemaw would say it,
meaning people in her day

got along just fine without any arms at all—
or iambic pentameter, for that matter,
lovers, hearses, democracy—

and if I was too busy sulking
as she sealed me in a crypt
for the rest of summer

with nothing for company
but a cask of Amontillado
and the mellow laughter of the dark,

then later, watching my wife and son
splash around our neighborhood pool,
I managed a tepid grin

for her slap on the hand to stop
being a big fat baby
and be grateful I hadn't broken

my writing hand or femurs or balls.
"It could be worse," I called to the lifeguard
slathering her silky arms with cocoa butter

just as a pigeon passed over
with that loaded look of fate
all pigeons have.

Ax

After breakfast a rain cloud
rumbles over our house like a large black cow
letting the universe know

no one has bothered to milk her.
Then more clouds pack in
until they are poor Londoners

jostling in the penny-pit
for a chance to pelt Iago with a moldy turnip
or a pint of ale,

though they'll have to settle
for a five-year-old
swearing he's put on clean underwear,

his father glowering
under an icy frown
and launching into a monologue

on the inconstancy of clouds—
how the frog at the living room window
will have given up its frogness

before reaching the kitchen door
and become Lizzie Borden
with that ax of hers

or Satan nudging Eve to the apple,
amateurs all
whose total lack of parenting is obvious

even to you, little thespian,
bending the arc of the world to your stage.
So, I hope you brought lunch,

because you're going to be awhile
listening to your old man drone about clouds,
this one a hawk

dragging its broken wing along the seashore,
that one a cowboy
on his way to Abilene,

smoking peacefully in the saddle
and singin'
yippee-ki-yo yippee-yo-ki-yay.

Ember

I was certain I had killed you,
corn spider
of the blood-orange bougainvillea,

when I strolled whistle-first
into the thousand and one silks
of your single summer,

somersaulting down the primrose path
like a man on fire
as you skedaddled in terror

off the rainy bleachers of my tongue;
but here you are again,
girding silence after silver silence

to a bandaged masterpiece,
which I would liken to a flaxen trestle
or a tapestry of medieval slaughter

were it not so abundantly clear,
as the wind stirs its lips
across the breath of your creation,

that you are a poet like the moth-white ape
swooning in the candlelight above,
you two burning your respective embers

to balm the night's black thirst
with all that language hungers to say:
Resistance is futile. Come.

Ode

To the little blue tape measure
with which I mark the wall
for an ousel etched in 1669—

the year Robert Boyle discovered phosphorous
and Samuel Pepys put his giant diary
out to pasture—praise

for the hundred harmonies it adds
to the measure of daily life
as opposed to the neighbor

who leant it years ago
and who never spoke to me again
after the sunny day she was thrown from a horse

and stripped naked in my front hallway,
so I could exam her broken collarbone,
with the addendum she loved me

and wanted to run away together,
at which point I carefully dressed her,
diagnosed a concussion,

and packed her off to the hospital with friends,
struck suddenly by the thought
that I had just starred

in the world's worst pornographic movie
unless what you're into—
what really gets you hot and bothered—

is a man in blue jeans and a loose grey sweater
strolling back to the long bookcase
in his living room

to stare thoughtfully and for a long time
at a small woodcut
of Himeji Castle in winter.

Son,

when the sun blooms into a red giant
five billion years from now,
gobbling up Mercury and Venus like wild radishes,

the last sentient life on Earth,
whether a gentle race of gardening bipeds
or a grumpy purple lichen

named Stan,
will have a front-row seat
to the absolute end of things,

the clouds running for cover, trees screaming,
oceans hot enough to poach an egg.
And that will take a lot of grit,

something like the grit your mother showed
laboring to bring you from her womb
until both your hearts began to wane

or the grit of the obstetrician
who drew you through her belly,
unwinding the cord

from your neck and wrists and feet,
or the grit you showed on the warming table,
five seconds old,

when you pushed yourself up
on both hands
and took a long, furrowed look

at the sapling world,
which for just that moment
was your sap of a father weeping.

Non-Toxic

I'm feeling pretty solid
about tonight's bedtime story
in which a little boy learns why superheroes

wear underpants outside their tights,
especially after last night's debacle
where the moon fell out of the sky,

obliterating not just the cow
who dared jump over it
but the cat and the fiddle, the little dog,

dish and spoon.
And no sooner have I switched off
the orange toadstool at his bedside table,

kissed his forehead, drawn the shade,
when through pale darkness
my son asks if he will die someday.

And it is good to have a suite
of plastic stars glowing on the wall,
a whorl of ice-tailed comets,

planets with many rings,
as a kind of usable answer
even if Kid-Socrates isn't ready to throw in the towel

and count some much-needed sheep,
wanting to hash out
what it means to be something

and what it means to be nothing
despite having a full day of preschool tomorrow,
a busy schedule

throwing sand at his friends and finger-painting dragons
or, should the Spirit so move him,
eating globs of non-toxic paste.

Beatrice

You had disappeared chirpily
down the tidy aisles
of this little Asian grocery

to find your favorite
good luck mushrooms
or a hairy, aphrodisiacal root,

so I sat at a lunch counter
tucked in back near the fire exit,
resting my elbows on its white linoleum

and sipping a cup of light green tea.
Plenty of time to gaze
at the tank of brackish water

in which a miracle of catfish was sardined,
whiskers madly flailing, starch-white bellies
squirming in and out of view.

One would no sooner shimmy up
against the slimed green glass
and stare out like some monolith of history

tugging Dante's crimson sleeve
before the maddened crowd
churned him back to the heart of darkness

to await the fillet knife, the batter, the frying oil.
And because of the burning purity
with which the open sky

married its blue to that morning's glory,
I despaired for all of us
stifling our own airy terrarium

as it goes on trumpeting its reveille
of seasons
and swirling us dutifully around the sun,

and I would have plunged headlong
into the smoky rings of my own abyss
had you not emerged just then,

raising a small black box in triumph
with no hint of what lay inside
beyond a sly, suggestive wink.

Apple

It's not every day the city
you serve as minor functionary
throws you the keys

to an unmarked police cruiser
with a Corvette engine
and paint black as the Madonna of Toulouse

to ferry yourself
from one official duty or another
until the humble mule cart

you're regularly assigned
is resurrected
at stupendous effort and expense;

but should you find yourself
by the curious interstices
of sloth and zeal,

which dictate life
in any thriving bureaucracy,
approaching the land-speed record

on a stretch of wildflowered highway
in wine country
and under sunny skies no less,

be ready for a grin
that hasn't stolen across your face
since the night it unfurled steaming green wings

and fled the ashes of your virginity,
or that other time some years later
when your beloved gave you a bite

of her apple
and the two of you were ushered from Paradise
by a giant angel

whose meaty hands on your shoulders
meant she was sorry
but had a man and kids and a job to do.

Featherbed

More than lungs full of pine tar and clouds,
I tell myself, scooping an overripe wino
into the belly of Medic 6,

more than blistered feet in an icy stream
or salmon snapping at the end of a line,
I'd love Liberty

to march across the open wounds of dusk,
sky of smog and fire,
torch raised for this mad white whale

in the sandwich sign
and rancid shower shoes,
this unwashed angel

wassailing on the razor's edge of mercy
with his beggar's cup and bellyful
of toxic sobriquets,

until some pugilistic commuter
surfaced long enough from the depths
of hump day vassalage

to leave him bleeding rivers in the street
and, because Boxcar Willie here is crawling
with Hepatitis A through Z,

put his unsuspecting wife at risk
for a slow, painful death
and their children,

who I pray are nothing more than figments
of my imagination,
two freckle-headed phantoms

passing a flashlight back and forth,
whispering their way through a ghost story
beneath the covers of a giant featherbed.

Reunion

I have nothing to do
for the rest of this autumn afternoon
but sit on an iron bench

at the leafy center of this park
with the sports section folded neatly on my lap,
a pebble on the shores of eternity,

a coin tossed in the fountain of time.
Let the man in the overcoat
chase his train down the crowded platform,

briefcase waving,
hat blown onto the rails,
or the woman watching a busy playground

behind the curtains of her bedroom window
send a sigh echoing
down the marble halls of memory.

Let the seasons ride their carousel,
the dog chase its tail,
Charon drag his rickety ferry

back and forth
across a river of forgotten tears,
and I will be here,

moss growing on the temple steps,
raindrop hanging from the stork's candle-flame bill.
When the sun has fallen

behind the General's famous bronze head,
the news stand locked its green shutters,
a friend will pick me up

in her tiny red sports car
and whisk us off to a bar
where many faces from the past

will drink too much
and laugh at our
sagging muscles and thinning hair

and, as the evening careens
from cocktails to shots, sing
the agony of child-rearing, the loss of religion,

marriages toppled like stacks of plates.
But for now it is enough to float
in the chapters of the present,

a bookworm
content with the music of his chewing,
a man playing both sides of the chess table,

lifting a Queen
between his thumb and forefinger
before sighing thoughtfully and letting her go.

Genome

Maybe because rain taps like a taxman at the window
or the coffee is blacker
than the velvety birth of the universe,

you call yours a prison
where God on the throne in Heaven,
with that stormy gaze of His

and beard of fluffy white clouds,
is one more knucklehead whittling away
a life sentence in Cellblock D.

So we switch to whiskey
and wait for the sun
to hurl golden javelins

as if the point of life is to live,
which it is, I say,
raising a small glass of fire

to my own little tenement
of questionable construction
whose thousands of strange characters

shape my journey from shadow
to stage to shadow,
a boy in white high tops

breakdancing on the roof, head-spinning
for a coop of pigeons
half-dreaming of the days

they were tyrannosaurs
or his kid sister
who knows all the secret places

beyond garden and fence
where the world runs to rushes and reeds,
skipping stones to let the frog

swimming for cover
and the egret hunting the frog
know they are not alone,

or to whisper her name
to the clear brown water,
because the water will tell everyone.

Principle

*"We have a principle that all poems about spring
are automatically disqualified."*
                              —Wislawa Szymborska

A great wooden horse
riddled with chicken-scratch roses
is hauled on blood-soaked oaken wheels

to the royal vineyard
where everyone has knocked off for the day
and skips naked

down rows of bright green chardonnay,
flashing hams
and smooching the family jewels

so hungrily
nobody hears the soft crunch
of forty elite snowmen

shifting in its belly,
the click-clack of wet stick fingers
tightening on candy cane spears.

Tchotchke

We've brought this on ourselves,
I whimpered,
as the bright young memoirist

pinned us against the ropes of his childhood
and worked us over
with a tally of teenage regrets,

we've brought this on our miserable,
godforsaken selves,
when there came from the Homeopathy aisle

the sharp odor of patchouli
followed by a tinkling of bells,
tiny bronze window bells, it turned out,

on a mobile of pencil-thin iron
a finchy angel held forth,
swishing prayerfully

towards the register
in cork sandals and swaths of turquoise hemp,
not unlike the ghost of some poor Wiccan

condemned to roam the Earth
for a life of general free-spiritedness
until the millstones of commerce

should grind themselves to furious dust,
which really could not come soon enough,
I bellyached, hearkening that tchotchke

like a prisoner at the bars
of his cell's small window
watching a caravan of fortune-tellers

juggle scimitars and hoops of fire
as they steered off the Silk Road one desert evening
to water their horses

and kidnap any curious children
from the barren edge
of that rain-colored town.

Surrender

The customer refreshment zone
of this sweeping dealership
nestled along the Interstate

like a tumor of the human spirit
is the worst place imaginable to mine
a cinderblock-thick history

of the Roman Empire's slow decline,
worse than the belly of an active volcano,
worse than a guillotine's

neckworn crook.
Not for any fault of the author's,
a laureled pillar knighted

for lighting bonfires in the brain,
but because of a chalkboard-sized television
bolted to the wall

and the talk show host therein
going bananas in a language
of arm flaps and rabbit shrieks,

flitting from one inanity to another,
like an unhinged cockatiel
some troubled child has set on fire,

so that any comprehension
of small-pox-riddled legionaries
perishing under Gothic clubs

in the black forests
of the western hinterlands
must now make room for Hollywood's

premiere pet hypnotherapist
strutting around in a loud scarf
and big white sunglasses,

giving his picks for the season's
trendiest canine sweaters,
and the fraying of Britannia

involve a celebrity physician
cooking heart-healthy margherita pizza
in an oven built from the ruins

of Hadrian's Wall.
There is nothing to do
but jam an emergency cigarette

in my stuttering lips
and hasten outside to the field next door
with the weight of the world

dragging down my shoulders
or, if not the world,
then at least the Oxford English Dictionary,

complete and unabridged,
slung across my back
like a medieval kite shield

as though the old historian,
last defender of the life of the mind,
and I, his rubber-kneed squire,

had walked out this morning
to reject the host's terms
of unconditional surrender,

much to the delight of her minions
smeared bodily with tomato sauce
and girdled in a patchwork armor

of chic dog sweaters—her hordes
who shall cut us to crow feed
before the sun has run out

on these soft native grasses,
the big bluestem, the sprangletop,
the blowing buffalo.

Scythe

There are these people called Danes
we have to thank
for Legos and the female condom,

people called the Dutch
without whom there'd be neither tulips
nor holding back the sea.

The Olmecs may strut
onto the stage of our affection
hand in hand with the Sumerians

to take a much-deserved bow
for the invention of writing,
while the Han Chinese

are waiting in the wings with their compass,
Hungarians the ballpoint pen,
Georgians wine.

But stuck in this warm plastic cube
beside the highway,
waiting out a blizzard

and watching a farmer with an orange hat
in the far distance
slog towards a snow-bound donkey

with a shotgun under his arm,
I wonder who to thank
for this cheeseburger,

which would still be a cheeseburger
centuries from now
were I to build a little church

and lay it in a golden tabernacle
for people of the future to behold;
still a cheeseburger

after people of the future
had tumbled to crumbs
with their superbrains and hoverboards;

still a cheeseburger
even after Art had disappeared
down its own rabbit hole

and Song buried its flute
where Death could never find it—
not that Death would be looking anyway,

zipping along with his hoverboard
on waves of killer sunset,
air-guitaring an otherwise useless scythe.

Chicxulub

If you're the man in the black
satin eye mask,
the child covered in peanuts,

or the lady with a scotch and soda
pooled in the crotch
of her red silk skirt,

then the hips of this flight attendant
as she ambles down the aisle
dispensing sustenance and luxury

must seem like Sherman over Georgia
or Hector smashing
through a wall of Grecian spears.

If by chance you're the unlovable slice
of greasy terminal pizza
lying face down on the carpet

or one of the unlucky schmucks
getting strafed
by a box of Junior Mints

jilted into the mix,
her big no-nonsense birthers
must seem like Salah-ad-Din

breaching the walls of Jerusalem,
an asteroid knocking the dinosaurs
off their high horse,

or Moby Dick
moseying through a cloud
of bright pink krill.

But to me, paralyzed
by a tiny glowing screen
on which a tiny hamster

is eating tiny burritos,
only to be rocked back to the miracle
of hurtling through the sky

at five hundred thirty-five miles per hour
in a tampon applicator with wings,
they are two baby elephants

gamboling under a blanket
of lemon yellow wool
their keeper has brought them

and so delighted in the nearness
of one another
they've forgotten they're anywhere

but a swath of sunny grassland savannah
broken here and there
by a lone acacia tree.

Passion

The wall beyond this window
is purpled in bursts
from the sprawling southern family,

Passifloraceae,
green with the sting of August
and helixed in honeybees

harvesting a thousand bruised nectaries
of this late wet-summer bloom,
droning with a timbre

honed by several million years
of outmaneuvering meteor strikes and ice ages,
wildfire, hungry bears, glyphosate.

And they will be droning still
tomorrow, a week from now, a century,
certainly after the asphalt gang

smoking and eating sandwiches
in the shade of my front oak
have finished laughing themselves silly

at a story the fat one told
about what his girlfriend
tried to do to him last night

with a cucumber
and how he outmaneuvered her
with a trick of the tongue

he guarantees will make any woman
forget all her troubles,
going so far as to demonstrate

his secret
with the remnants of his ham and cheese
to applause so thunderous

even I have to run to the window,
drawing back the curtain
to see how the thing is done.

Texas

Like a million masons mortared
in the Great Wall of China,
or the charcoal-spitting Da Vincis of Lascaux,

the names are lost to posterity
of the studio musicians who laid down
the background theme

for an infomercial
spurring the small herd of this waiting room
to a paradise of tax havens

once the aegis
of narco-saints and capitalist pigs,
but now open to the rest of us

penny-pinching chuckleheads,
me with my jam shorts
and root surface sensitivity,

a disheveled pensioner gumming his last tooth
like a dream-laden dog,
two toddlers

by the potted fern
pounding the tar out of one another
over a Where's Waldo book

because they long to find Waldo
the way stardust longs for sentience
and sentience longs for gods,

the way narrative longs for audience
and audience longs for Art,
the way their pretty mother,

with rings of Saturn under her eyes,
longs for a hot bath and a nap,
for her stoop-shouldered lover

to air the wine tonight and lay down
a miracle for dinner,
his Texas chili, his chicken Provençal.

Annals

And the man sat.
And the tree was happy.
—Shel Silverstein

But after a while the wind blew,
and deep in her roots the tree recalled
green canopy, white blossoms,

her great black limbs
groaning in sunlight
or waltzing with a storm.

And the man sitting there,
cradling the anvil of self-pity,
felt suddenly like an anvil himself.

Birds sang how the tree,
once orphaned to glacial darkness,
had spread her rings across a century,

but she could hear only
the patter of small white fists
pounding her trunk with regret.

"I love you," she began to say,
"I have always loved you,"
when the man let fly,

sighing with violent pleasure.
And somewhere inside the tree
a door shut,

glass shattered, waters broke
at the bottom of a well.
And here—as I float the Buffalo

on a cold Spring morning
watching a man the shape of a cracker barrel
flick one cigarette butt after another

into the kingfishers and cricket frogs—
here is where I would understand
if the tree grew teeth and ate the old man

leaving his bloody ear in the mud
like a calling card,
where I would withhold judgment,

maybe even cheer a little
and wave a bright pennant on a stick,
if she pried herself

from the Earth's wet suck
and wriggled off, a dichotomous octopus
hellbent on sating her newfound

lust for muscle and bone,
slouching
towards the annals of human horror

by way of fiery climax
in the ashes of Houston
or the Lake of Innisfree.

Atropos

It would be ridiculous
wanting to lie down with any of the Fates
in sweaty conflagration,

let alone the one
pressing the crotch of her fabled scissors
to the scarlet thumping of a pulse,

but that is precisely what I wished to do
after watching a trench cave suddenly
under an excavator this morning,

the operator pirouetting free
in adrenaline-drenched magnificence
before all fifty tons

could mash him like a golden wonder,
a poor man's russet, a Jersey sweet.
Be it salacious or suicidal,

something in the red dust cloud
mushrooming from the crater
and the pale-faced drivers

screaming silently
behind their tempered windows,
something in the guy's abraded fingers

grasping at the earthen lip
made me want to ease the blood-
colored shears from Her weary hands

and slide Her starry toga to the floor,
the kind of desire, I thought later,
pruning the low-hung leaves from every

bird-drop sunflower crowding the garden,
that might land you
a bowl of tepid hemlock

in a stormy court of ancient Athens
or the grin of a discerning reader
on an ordinary Wednesday

in the twenty-first century
with highs expected in the 70s
and sunshine likely through the afternoon.

Cup

Two stories come to mind
when I scoop you up on the walk to school
and find your lip is trembling,

because it's cold, and your orange
hunter's cap has disappeared.
Once upon a time your great-grandfather

sent me out after a hard freeze
to rid his yard of fallen mulberries.
If I got them all, he promised

dragon's gold, a flaming sword, the cup of life.
And a witch to gobble me up
if a single one got by.

The grass was pale sky
and scarlet starlight,
the belly of the witch so black

it took me years to find the mulberry
hiding in the old man's pocket.
Once upon a time, after a deep snow,

I trod a white river
with a dog named for a god
who'd run ahead and plunged through

a blue hole in the ice.
And this story
is about neither the god nor the dog

but the blue hole in the ice
all men become to one another.
Dangling you by your matchstick arms,

I quake like a giant
and swear I'll throw you in a pot
and cook you for my supper.

You peal with laughter
and plant the hero's kiss
on my morning shadow.

I am your father again,
swallower of children,
devourer of worlds.

Wall

You were talking about something
through the black thunders
of this poorly caffeinated morning,

the resurgence of global tyranny
or your sore left boob,
Time unpainting the house.

Then you slapped the table
and sloshed off in a yellow slicker,
bright blue umbrella

fending sheets of rain,
leaving me
to mull your frozen proclamation

that talking to me is like talking to a wall.
No doubt you meant the mired bricks
down some wharf district alley

where nobody shovels the fish kill
or spellchecks the graffiti,
a Martian Rushmore

with four of my heads
staring vacantly toward Pluto
or some pockmarked monolith

where cigarettes twirl
ass over teakettle
from the grins of blindfolded men.

But now that the clouds are broken,
the black branches fleeced of ice,
now that you've surely reached the meadow

high above our refuge
and broken a pleasant sweat,
I hope I am less

the slab of weathered grudges
holding Pyramus back from Thisbe's arms
and more the crack they whisper through,

more the stack of field stones
raised to mark an empire's end
and built so low

any old turtle might lumber over,
citizen newly minted,
refugee flying to the wild unknown.

Paris

I know there's more to this city
than a budget hotel room
on the icy outskirts of Charles de Gaulle Airport,

many notable arches to pass solemnly under,
myriad bridges for the dropping
of brokenhearted sighs,

but having been liquefied
by twenty-three hours
on the killing floor of global flight logistics

because the gold market infarcted
and it's raining bankers
or the Siberian Traps just erupted

and to all a goodnight,
this complementary 64 ft^2
I have until sunrise to call home

might as well be the beaches of Monaco
or a palace on the Moon.
Granted, I'm 3½ miles from the heart

of Western Liberalism,
coffee I'd backflip into a burning building for,
and the splayed fingers of Olympia

shielding that famous muff of hers
from the daggers of my slack-jawed gaze,
but tonight I'll settle for a liter

of vending machine red
and this floor-to-ceiling shower
of pellucid acrylic

hogging half the room
and spiraled like a shell
so that slouching towards its wet, hot center

is like ambling backwards
down the dim gallery of History
with its many scenes of Beauty and Horror

to a simpler era
when the streets were running lava
and our kinfolk swung cantaloupe-

sized knuckles at anything pea-brained enough
to challenge them
for King of the Mountain.

Transformer

Water scald and soap scour,
shoulders scolding
and simoleons in the bank, I am the First Man

breathing easy,
tuning his pulse to an ice storm
pelting the windows,

parade of tin can tinkerers,
arrows off a cloud of raised bronze shields,
when a pole transformer up 17th

suffers a fiery loss of faith
and the house blinks into primeval darkness—
not exactly an existential crisis

to write home about,
at least not compared to the tiny apocalypse
building steam in the laundry room

where a high-watt star has winked out
leaving a brood of chicks on their cardboard planet
to worry the Void

in a chorus of adorable peeps.
What'll *we* do, I wonder,
steering their good ship

close enough to the mantle
to carry them through the night,
when our own blazing center follows suit,

knowing at this molten hour,
as the oceans devolve to anoxic guacamole,
there are labs white hot

with women and men
racing to coax their selves
into better elements and blast off to infinity,

and a mere 800,000 centuries left
to pour a midnight whiskey
and run my fingers through your dreaming hair.

Mattress

Just in case we forgot
how to lie down on one
in the time it took

to ferry Old Faithful to the curb
and forage our fair city's corn-frocked
outermost rings

for this sturdy virgin,
directions are waiting to explain the whole business
when we slash her elastic chains

and unleash this pillow-topped beast
to free-range
in our airy orgasmatarium,

a little two-paned comic starring a stickman
first shown unrolling his mattress
and then lying down on it,

I guess instead of setting it ablaze
and tossing it off a bridge,
which can only mean, love,

there are people out there
desperately
in need of Step 3

where two stick figures
speak universally
in the Unruly Unicorn position,

the position of Rescue Dolphin,
Bald Eagle Guitar Solo or Birthday Dogs
while breakfast dishes clitter

and plaster cockles off the walls,
giving their new best friend a run for her money—
pleased, clearly,

they didn't go with an acrylic dinette set
or, gods be praised,
that pair of wicker chairs.

The Aristocrats

Forty years in the biz have made him
a bird lover,
so that his mind will often wander

away from the man with a bowling ball
hanging off his coin purse
or the lady smoking fifty cigarettes

with her snatch,
his heart will put on galoshes and a bright yellow coat,
tramping past the dog on the unicycle

juggling dogs on unicycles,
a chimpanzee dressed up as Hamlet,
a cat laying down the end solo of *Hotel California*

with mystifying ease
to study a wet black branch
where a sparrow marries coffee straws

to maple twigs and pine
or a blue jay
roots a fruit fly

from under his cornflower wing.
He'll even take the pigeon
with a cigarette butt

dangling rebelliously off her tangerine beak
for the crumpled pack of menthols
tucked in his own breast pocket.

So it comes as no surprise
that he's already high
above the sandhills of Nebraska,

wind sifting cottonseed from his wet-slate feathers
and clouds like kraken
winkled with hints of the coming sea,

when a plainclothes family of six
who might be selling orthodoxy or apple pie
comes in from the rain one afternoon,

their mastiff shaking out his fur on the rug
as the father extends a warm, naked paw
saying, "Mister, have we got an act for you."

Doe

The early birds have unfolded all the tables
and clothed them in gingham
checkered red and white

before the mist has burned away,
and by the time the sun has hung
its shingle of blue sky

to signal another day of summer,
they've brewed a Buddha-shaped urn of coffee,
raised a crop of jelly donuts,

and iced down plenty of beer
for the Johns and Janes
brought by bad luck or tragedy

to this green valley of anonymity,
the unmissed and missing,
the sorrowed ciphers of our sometime world

trading blue jokes and firm handshakes,
embrace after warm embrace,
taking this day to celebrate themselves

with cold fried chicken and potato salad,
to spin the loom of gossip
or spring from a mossy dock

into water dark and cold as a bruise.
And long after moonrise,
every Doe from the far reaches of spaceship Earth

lays out blankets
to watch fireworks cannonade
from the next valley over

where the Unknown Soldiers
romp through their yearly barbeque,
the whole party drifting towards sleep

or stargazing or sweet mischief in the trees.
A campfire flickers in a fieldstone ring
and a Jane runs her fingers

through the sandy curls of a small John
with his head in her lap,
his eyelids pale marble

as she sings a soft lullaby
about holding the hand of a little boy like him
who called her *Mother*.

Ox

No hard feelings,
Passport Office vending machine,
for jamming

when I feed you a dollar,
for holding that bag of M&Ms
like a field mouse

balled in a marsh hawk's claw
even after I kick you
where I think your heart should be

and call you something worse
than Satan's white hot asshole,
making the constable

hug his muffin top with laughter
and my marriage tick
five seconds closer to nuclear midnight.

I get it,
because when my son surfaced
from his cereal bowl this morning,

milk streaming down his chin
and a cornflake pasted on his nose,
to ask for the first

of today's five hundred stories,
the revolving door between
my mouth and imagination

got so mobbed
with dinosaurs and cowboys,
robots, aliens, and talking bears

all vying
to be the center of a universe,
that what fumbled through was mishmash

about a dad staring into his coffee
like a plough ox studying cold, wet mud.
And maybe that is your problem, too,

wanting to give and give and give,
not a few measly beads
of candy-coated chocolate,

but mountains of caramel, lakes of caffeine,
perhaps even the golden tickets
we require

to revive our dogged spirits
on the white hot beaches of Greece,
maenads libating us

with magical frozen alcohol
while the blue Aegean
pours honey-tongued lies about the gods.

To the Blind Woman Who Bails from Her Boyfriend's Car Traveling North on Interstate 35 at 70 MPH Causing a Massive Pileup as Cold Rain Falls in Late September

for Fred

There are a thousand ways to begin a journey.
A muffled chirping
leads you to the porch one steamy morning

where a python is curled peacefully
under a purple lawn chair,
its belly shaped like your pet canary, Fred.

Or, boarding a ship for Ithaca, you notice
green salt waves
wine-dark with another city's heroes

and stop your infernal singing.
You rescue a leprechaun rooting
around your trash cans like a raccoon

and soon have a pot of gold
to get that spaceship in the garage
going again.

Or one wind-whipping Wednesday night
you leap from a pea-green Trans Am
because your love is a ham-fisted Rumi,

and the trucker who sees you
unspooling down the fry-pan asphalt
like a panicked smack of pink moon jellies

or silly putty come suddenly to life
jackknifes thirty tons of candy bars
bound for the children of Kentucky,

gashing his saddle tanks
and gushing a spring of diesel
unto the aquifers of life,

until my best people stem it
and pull your femurs back in place
that you might wake to know

love is the python
wrapping not around your songbird
but your song.

Oratory

To tell you, painter's bucket, life ain't fair—
where you wait
in weeds no streetlamp troubles

for your owner to finish another trick
and ablute with your moonlit waters—
would be like telling the sperm

runneling down his pale bruised thighs
to hitch their tiny wagons to a star
or the woman in the trash bag

and hospital bracelets
telling the world's last payphone
to fuck a duck

that things fall apart;
but, then again, we are a people
keen to feed kindergarteners

to our Second Amendment,
so it's clear some things bear repeating
like

horses
eating
sunrise on icy persimmons

creek trickle trilling
the lovers' slide of continents
over Earth's iron heart,

or the words a kid stumbles over
on Recitation Day,
the short protest poem

she stayed up late singing to her mirror
until its loss and jubilation
had come across just so,

so that here in fourth period English
she gives her heart a chance to gather up
the pages of its first symphony

and, with a bow
to the crowd's good humor,
pluck its baton from a French horn's bell.

Big Gulp

The garden is monarchs
resting ochre petals
450 million wingbeats from the milkweed

meadows of Vermont,
guzzling nectar from rainbow lantana
before chancing on

to the oyamels of Michoacán,
and atop the blue Adirondack chair
where I'm flopped

muzzling a silty last coffee sip
and stubbing out a smoke,
a roly-poly treks over my big toe

busily defying a cold, dark universe
as its trilobite kin were doing
450 million years ago

in the Ordovician's warm, shallow seas
when Great Mother squat on her knees
and bore the Appalachians,

leaving them to litter the ditches
of suburban Cincinnati
amongst the Big Gulp cups and thistle,

not so far from Her oldest fossil beds
Christians bury under creation museums
with the same gusto

they summoned to burn the classical world,
opening the door for one Archbishop
of Armagh to wander on stage

in the 17th century and decide the world began
on October 23rd, 4004 BC,
right about the time his god got going

as a Canaanite shaker of volcanos
and exactly 6082 years ago today
before you came along, lover,

to grace this thin green skein we call
the biosphere,
that is to say, "Happy Birthday!"

Isorenieratene

For the next fifteen minutes,
thanks to a skywriter
tunneling like a silver termite

through the sky's dissembling blue,
anybody looking up
as I am

from this orchard of spindly figs
in bleak midwinter
will know that Jerry digs Frida

and would very much like
her hand in marriage,
to the extent Jerry commissioned

his whole proposal be whorled
in a heart of white paraffin smoke.
Let us wish the lovebirds well

and assume Frida trembles
with joy
as she gazes out a taxi window

or steps from her bakery,
tears
tracing down her flour-dusted cheeks,

that is,
unless Frida happens to be a geologist,
in which case she probably sees

the breath of Madame Pele
tra-la-la-ing from the metal anus
of anthropic hubris,

one more tiny sledgehammer
banging on the world's thermostat
and spearheading our nosedive

back to the sloppy green oceans of yore,
which Jerry may not be able
even to imagine

let alone troubleshoot or vote wisely over,
or maybe Frida's a Big Oil exec
diddling herself in a high glass tower

over Jerry's rather frontal
public display of affection—
in which case, Jerry,

no need to get your act together,
you just keep on bein' Jerry, man,
you're good to go.

Hello

You write the most surprising things
across the salvaged midnight
of an old slate chalkboard in our hall,

things like "Paint the house,"
or "Paint the damn house,"
or, my personal favorite,

"Don't even think about pussy
until you paint this fucking house."
"Well, let's just see about that,"

I tell our mean-eyed cat,
scheming over a poem
that will send your chastity belt

clattering to the floor,
and flip-flopping out the door
with *Anna Karenina* and a six-pack,

a slug of zinc sunbathing on my nose,
making for our favorite swimming hole—
but not without leaving a note of my own

so that the first thing you see
coming in from work
will be a big cartoon schlong,

worry-free and waving hello
from the shadows of suppertime
where once grew

the climbing vines and airy curlicues
of your perfect cursive,
that most endangered of arts

destined to go
the way of the ivory bill and passenger pigeon,
the way of the dodo.

Acknowledgments

Grateful acknowledgment is made to the following publications where many of the poems in this collection first appeared:

Aperçus Quarterly: "Americano," "Atropos," "Europa," "Featherbed,"
   "La Jolla," "Modern"
The Chattahoochee Review: "Cup," "Scythe"
Cold Mountain Review: "Annals"
Concho River Review: "Ax"
december: "Beatrice," "Dunkleosteous"
Good Works Review: "Apple," "Passion," "Physical"
North American Review: "Spandex"
TriQuarterly: "Icon," "Surrender"
West Texas Literary Review: "To the Blind Woman Who Bails from Her
   Boyfriend's Car Traveling North on Interstate 35 at 70 MPH Causing
   a Massive Pileup as Cold Rain Falls in Late September"

About FutureCycle Press

FutureCycle Press is dedicated to publishing lasting English-language poetry books, chapbooks, and anthologies in both print-on-demand and Kindle ebook formats. Founded in 2007 by long-time independent editor/publishers and partners Diane Kistner and Robert S. King, the press incorporated as a nonprofit in 2012. A number of our editors are distinguished poets and writers in their own right, and we have been actively involved in the small press movement going back to the early seventies.

The FutureCycle Poetry Book Prize and honorarium is awarded annually for the best full-length volume of poetry we publish in a calendar year. Introduced in 2013, our Good Works projects are anthologies devoted to issues of universal significance, with all proceeds donated to a related worthy cause. Our Selected Poems series highlights contemporary poets with a substantial body of work to their credit; with this series we strive to resurrect work that has had limited distribution and is now out of print.

We are dedicated to giving all of the authors we publish the care their work deserves, making our catalog of titles the most diverse and distinguished it can be, and paying forward any earnings to fund more great books.

We've learned a few things about independent publishing over the years. We've also evolved a unique, resilient publishing model that allows us to focus mainly on vetting and preserving for posterity poetry collections of exceptional quality without becoming overwhelmed with bookkeeping and mailing, fundraising activities, or taxing editorial and production "bubbles." To find out more about what we are doing, come see us at www.futurecycle.org.

The FutureCycle Poetry Book Prize

All full-length volumes of poetry published by FutureCycle Press in a calendar year are considered for the annual FutureCycle Poetry Book Prize. This allows us to consider each submission on its own merits, outside of the context of a contest. Too, the judges see the finished book, which will have benefitted from the beautiful book design and strong editorial gloss we are famous for.

The book ranked the best in judging is announced as the prize-winner in the subsequent year. There is no fixed monetary award; instead, the winning poet receives an honorarium of 20% of the total net royalties from all poetry books and chapbooks the press sold online in the year the winning book was published. The winner is also accorded the honor of being on the panel of judges for the next year's competition; all judges receive copies of all contending books to keep for their personal library.

www.ingramcontent.com/pod-product-compliance
Lightning Source LLC
Chambersburg PA
CBHW070002100426
42741CB00012B/3103